Fighting Exile:
A Heart's Return to Montana

Fighting Exile:
A Heart's Return to Montana

Terry Brix

Kelsay Books

Cover design: Shay Culligan
Cover photograph: Jeri Childs, Seattle Professional Photographer

Library of Congress Control Number: 2018952986

ISBN: 978-1-949229-08-0

Kelsay Books
Aldrich Press
www.kelsaybooks.com

To Susan
Always

Acknowledgements

Grateful acknowledgement is made to the editors of the following publications where these poems or earlier versions of them first appeared:

Antioch Review: "Pulp Town"
Bellowing Ark: "Last Great Grandfathers" "Two Dot, Montana"
Blackmail Press: "Slide in the Direction of Make Believe," "High Desert Dance," "Railroad Track Guitar," and "A Tapeworm For All Seasons"
Blueline: "Passing Shadows"
Branches Quarterly: "Explaining Montana Cut Hay"
Chiron Review: "Fields Station Café"
Evansville Review: "Bar-Coded Life"
Front Range: "A Rugged West—a Fragile Menagerie"
Iodine Poetry Journal: "288 Months Pregnant"
Lucid Rhythms: "So Many Things Forgotten"
Main Channel Voices: "Departure of Parts"
New Rag Rising: "The Gaming Fields"
New Verse News: "Small Town Check-Up"
NFSPS 2010 William Stafford Memorial Award, Honorable Mention: "Simple Subtraction"
North American Review: "Boneless Nights"
Prairie Wolf Press Review: "Previews of Coming Attractions"
Rattlesnake Review: "What Day?"
Seasons of Change: "Bunkhouse Love"
Sidereality: "Junked"
Small Brushes /Adept Press: "Tambourine Day"
Thunder Sandwich: "Loading Chute"
Thunder Sandwich: "Road Kill Past"
Wired Art: "My Paloose Son Sleeps"

Special thanks to Playa at Summer Lake, Oregon. I received a one-month poetry residency in 2012 which was the start of the *Fighting Exile* collection.

Contents

Montana Threads

I was born pre-threaded. Green threads of emerging spring
wheat—blades, bow tying around melting snow and
purple-white, peek-a-boo spring rooster tails.

August wheat straw stubble, gold twine mats around Fresno
Lake. A Hill-County-size landscape painting with a topaz
water center, rippling like only cool blue in autumn tan.

Beaver Creek carded and wove me into Bears Paw pines—a
water-bark amalgam man as rare as Sasquatch
between unicorn and dinosaur—top on any extinction list.

Thread so strong yanks a boy into a man, man to creator.
Twist-woven Missouri blue-green and Fort Benton cottonwood
fluff to ropes, St. Louis long, Sidney and Gardner coiled.

When at loose ends anywhere, any hint of Montana
strings up and tugs my heart, threads me home.

Brandings

At ten, I press my head up against
chicken wire fence, watch hens scratch.
So intent, patterns iron into my forehead.
Wear a band of hexagons, a chain-mesh headdress,
twisted wire designs—pressure on skin tattoos.

In seconds I was shot by geometry—snowflake
symmetry and benzene ring chemical structures.
Initiated into a secret society while watching
hens cluck over beetles, cracked corn.

I press up close to you, feel hot passion rivets
from nipples & tongue press on me, imprint me.
Go around wearing a big satisfied grin. Rustled
by love, invisibly branded. Can't see skin forehead
marks. Good news, all brandings match my clothes.

Two Dot, Montana

The town is a bar
framed by central Montana.
"Easy to find, hard to leave,"
slogan catch phrase.

Think of our two dots,
the you and then the me.
Separating then meeting,
close as kiss-shared breath.

Shortest distance between us
not a straight anything.
Three marriages and still counting.
Six children stopped counting.

You were not easy to find,
you are impossible to leave.
Like the name Two Dot—two
periods and the one sentence of us.

We Go Blind

Above Pipestone Pass east of Butte a night
hawk soars, back-lit by the Milky Way—
non-onrushing galaxy headlights.

Below, kilowatt highway and neon streets,
rhinestone bulbs reflect on wet asphalt—
jewels of reflected star light.

Beneath the assault of beauty by neon, white-hot
tungsten, artificial light tortures Montana
like Levi Jeans stapled to a lover's hips.

Dark earth of Montana fights back, but
momentarily blinded by long, bright streets.
Montana dark buckles into progress.

Champagne corks pop. Bright light towns
take our dark away. We go blind.

Took Them for Granted

Fell in love first with cuddly Bears Paw,
close-at-hand & Teddy-Bear-Havre girl next
door. Classmates learn language of love on
front-room couches, Chevy back-seat Braille.

College courses all attractive, too many choices,
multiple curriculums within one female major.
Dated Beartooths, Crazies, Bridgers, Spanish Peaks.
No permanent peak girl—just passing foothills.

Ended decades married to the Cascades,
flirted with, flew to & around foreign ranges.
Got as far west as Japan's Fuji and Mt. Asao,
east to Finland, south to African Drakensburgs.

Searched for 'the one' mountain my whole life.
Scaled heights, traversed escarpments, gasped at
high altitudes, and inhaled iced aspen breezes.
Took them all for granted like gravity or speed of light.

Loved mountains have poof vanished.
Entire ranges became ghosts one winter night.
Affection wrung out between dusk and dawn,
paper thin, crumpled black & white good byes.

Trying something dramatically different now—
record mountain range of my wife day by hand,
make geologic maps of her lobes, poems of lips,
tattoo my dreams on the topography of hips.

So Many Things Forgotten

So many things I never knew about my father,
so many songs to which I have forgotten words.
Can't even hum the decades-distant melodies.
Remember those hands of a surgeon,
camouflaged in diesel fuel, box car grease.
He could tie trout flies with two fingers.
Ended uncoupling grain cars, preparing
syringes for self-injecting insulin.

Early morning arrivals, midnight departures,
wail of Great Northern rail yard trains pleading
for father's attention like a needy lover,
luring him like crying steel-footed sirens.
Pleasant benefit was that Xmas could come anytime.
All father did was call Santa, set the new day.

Long Sunday, old '53 Nash drives to grandma's.
Great Falls old country raisin-sauced tongue,
marinated rabbit, old family feuds stewed.
His guilt about not supporting his own family
growing like a cancer on the way home
until it python-ed his stamina, then crushed him.

Times I went to Whitefish in the caboose
with his god-like part-the-seas-commands,
for trains, crews, sidetracks, and crossings.
Diesel-fuel smells mixed with Old Spice,
Burma Shave and toil coiled around him.

The way he just worked year after year
on the locomotive trireme galley—a
slave pulling oars through the Hi-Line
wheat fields, a prophet in weather so cold

words froze, fell, cutting lips that uttered them.
Memory the bow, Montana the resonating body.
Maybe not so many things forgotten after all.

Loading Chute

Howe, Arco, Carey—Montana, Idaho,
I guess. Can't remember in the blur of
towns, bar named The Loading Chute.
Never been there before, but know it.

Dreams get stock-yarded,
stampede of frenzied feelings,
drinks calm, funnel me down
to a one-way chute.

Nights of drinking slaughtering
everything I love, care about,
complete with the coupe de grace
hangover bullet hole behind the ear.

Then I chute-up at the next bar,
load-up with a shooter or six-pack,
wait for the final Upton Sinclair *Jungle*,
skull-plunger 'thunk' making movement-meat.

The Loading Chute, I pass by at sixty,
battlefront, guerilla war zone, spies. Escape.
Carnage disappearing in my rear view mirror.
Ahead—ambushes for me—tomorrow, forever.

Listening to the McKenzie

Never was a river listener.
Milk River sloughish, milky,
murked by Havre, Montana like a
mute sneak on the run and hide.
Living with the clear McKenzie is
like studying a new language. Not
Norwegian, organic chemistry,
just a lemon peel of utter silence
twisted until it flavors your ears.
When the water hits the rocks,
hear the tone of the pardon me.
I'll just scoot over here to the left.
Water encompasses roots, sprouts
like listening to bread kneaded.
All that preparation for spring growth.
Operation overheard, bank sobbing, a
clump of reeds surgically removed.
Joy of an autumn leaf on rapids
taking a carnival ride, gleeing.
Listen to mid-stream currents,
liquid athletes talking bubbling trash
practicing one-upmanship, teamwork
streaming, exercising night and day
waiting for the next big game—rain.
Watch the heron look in the water.
Bows her head in recognition, hands me
my ears a quick river translation.

Past Loading

Orphaned at twenty-nine. Mother dead of a self-
inflicted rifle shot. Two years after Dad.
Montana generations seem high speed blended.
Snow, Milk River water tinged with family O+
blood, railroad muscle and Durum wheat soil.

Can't look at Beaver Creek without seeing
Dad fly-fishing over a grass-shaded hole.
Petunias (any continent) conjure Mother—
pink, blue, white petal tones, hint of her gray.
Lilacs in Helsinki—become 1026 5th Street lilacs.

I look at Saddle Butte, see my parents
side-by-side with a huge gap between them,
fighting tooth and nail. Kept the saddle nearby.
Wasn't a bad thing to clutch, cling onto having
'shoot-em up,' wild bronco and Brahma parents.

Parents never missed any supposed marriage
bad times. Hey, they liked frosty anniversaries.
Nah! Their idea of a good time was sharing a hate.
If alive, children, grandkids (8), greats (11) might
have been draws—curiosity breaks between knife fights.

Always wanted to get their take on how did
Vietnam swallow my brother Robert whole,
choked on him, and spit him back out?

Too late now—tamping down the gunpowder of
family, waiting for another spark.

Pulp Town

Town smells like barbecue & farts,
rancid steam & dump burning smoke,
old perfume on sex sweated bodies.
Clouds look like clouds but are disguised,
drugged, low & close like a poisoned pillow,
ozone holes tethered over main street,
part of a killing jar for a way of life,
a toxic Macy's parade with no crowds.

This is the kind of timber town
that fells trees, ends up with stumps,
every log out has part of a man crucified
thumb here tacked to cedar bark,
arm pinned on a Douglas fir,
leg sandwiched, pressed into plywood,
stenciled pleas scratched on the log ends,
codes, messages crying for help, but
foresters minimum wage has been paid,
profit made, 911 calls, no answers at all.

This kind of paper town chips, whittles
at you day by day, pulps, pulp liquors you
until like hate it digests muscle, soul,
consumes everything but the redneck.
Takes upright, ends with thin 3-D life
flattened to one-inch-by-three epitaph.
Even the bark, slash and saw whine
into Presto logs, Kingsford charcoal
briquettes dying, dead cremated alive
driving around in a 4x4 six-liter urn.
We all live in pulp town—our capital.

Boneless Nights

What I like about a Montana night—
nothing like day with anatomy precise edges,
dangling limbs, hefty torsos, grimaces & staring anger,
dirty mirror smudges, smoked and broken horizons.

My night is smooth and continuous ebony silk
blind eyes while fingers slide along skin, tactile-only
distinctions. The night bra lace and sea breeze. Dark
chocolate pudding rubbed between thumb and forefinger.

Day big-legged skyscrapers, industrial plants,
their iron femurs crushed, high rise vertebrae
apartments pulverizing. Corroding Jello-ed forms,
beached whalebone cities bleach to dusk.

Finger telephone poles, power line webs,
Smokestacks. City asphalted streets, avenues
stop-lighted hot irons. Every hand fisted, clenched.
Heat sizzles from concrete. Withering dance of fumes.

My brow imagines invisible cool night strands,
longs for silent black surfaces punctured with stars.

Snaking interstates, crosshatched county road nets,
asphalt flypaper trapping rush hour commuters, and
trains of cars turned to octane intestines.
Goodbye foul rumbled, heard and smelled.

Montana night takes the body of the day and
surgically removes the bones.

Slide in the Direction of Make Believe

Three Forks, Montana, an area, a little town.
Madison, Jefferson and Gallatin tributaries,
snake, slide and caucus together. Stream delegates,
eternal triangle-ing, yet voted unanimously for Missouri.

Havre, a straight town with only two directions—east and west.
Trains chug in and out, hibernating briefly like grizzly bears.
Streets and avenues cross hatch, the Bears Paw Mountains
sit like an exclamation point at the end of a very good book.

Choteau and Dupuyer backs nestle up against the Rockies, like
exhausted lovers staggering in the heat produced by alcohol-
ignited Native Americans trapped on the Blackfeet
        Reservation.
Montana facts—slide in the direction of make believe.

A Rugged West—a Fragile Menagerie

Imagining the West, we conjure up feelings of tough,
wild, free, and powerful like swilling testosterone, Smirnoff,
gunpowder cocktails. Marlboro Man look-alikes,
Skoal jowlers, ash and butt it and open ground spittoon it.
Men drink Coors and how-fresh-is-your-beer Budweiser,
leaving bars in a state of stale and side roads with fresh
pop-top urine. Hunters arsenal-up with rifles, automatics,
six-packs, leaving cartridges and aluminum cans strewn
amongst suffering rump-shot mule deer carcasses.
We toast the wild horses and wide-open spaces, while
bit-by-bit we grind this ecological menagerie into grit.

High Desert Dance

Today high desert is putting on the first dance of spring.
Noon lit cumulous strobe by slowly. Males grey cloud by.
Young female mountains ring the dance floor,
their dresses hemmed with junipers hued with sage.
I am just a small boy today admiring the men overhead,
looking up the varied skirts to glimpse what I have only
imagined. Birds direct the wind in the former dry
lake bed. Sections of land, an undulating dance floor
pulse. Keep beat—the left lane, right lane, a highway shuffle.
My ears and heart have heard and been to this dance before.
It must be a top ten all time hit for souls that like High
Desert Dance—mountain mind rock & cloud billow roll.

The Gold Filter

Days of summer, hammered inlaid gold, thinned
by heated blows of July-August down beat sun.

Acres of August Montana stubble wheat straw
like mini-metal pipe organs blow mirage baubles.

Auric leaves tambourine flutter filter sunsets,
dawns of all white clouds striated purples and crimsons.

An odd kingdom where spring green kisses, breath of love,
transform into the color of bankable heart wealth.

I wander autumn asphalt roads, dirt roads, rail sides.
Single trees seem like savings bank for hanging kisses.

Gold trees, wheat fields, adjacent winter wheat sown.
Row upon row glowing. Fall the gold filter.

A Tapeworm for All Seasons

Montana creek beds loop back and forth
knot themselves like intestines.
The creeks are bowels of the prairie
slowly digesting the countryside.
Gnawing at the banks—a fickle watery
dog, chewing on flat-land bone.
Flow agitates, torments, the creek bottom,
takes sedimentary peace, makes silt
turmoil. Run-off depletes the county host,
flushes muscle of the land to the Gulf. Creek
innards, banks—a tapeworm for all seasons.

Explaining Montana Cut Hay

Cut hay lying in windrows is the sun speaking through your nose.
It is the smell of cut promises neatly heaped and stacked at day's
    close.
Cut hay is small broken moonbeams casting a menthol mint chill,
freezing the fragrance history of plant life chattered, echoed, now
    still.
Rifled Ponderosa needles shot and breezed through clouds of sage,
targeted into dollops of honey dusted further with goldenrod glaze.
There is the subtle distant dank swamp and seaweed brew,
hint of old fish, charred cedar forest and a hot sweaty crew.
That is just the start of explaining the smell of Montana cut hay,
drinking a cup of water knowing it's connected someway to
    Hudson Bay.

Search for Loneliness

Airport security asks for passport, boarding
pass, return ticket. Headed to another country
where I don't know a soul. They search bags,
ask about sharp objects. I don't tell them about you.
They don't ask about razor edged words,
landmines of divorce, old trip-wired habits.

I'm pulled aside. A guard wand scans me. No
embedded slugs, magnetic anal capsules or firearms.
Shoes inspected as though I were a clandestine,
terrorist warhorse instead of a hobbling plow horse.

TSA searches for contraband, dangerous
objects, watches for suspicious behavior.
I ask, "Have you found any loneliness?"

He stares at me blankly, then says, "Why would
anyone ask that question unless they *were* lonely?"

I don't tell him that loneliness is a deadly weapon.
I carry it, carefully concealed in my poetry.

In Sound Drowned

I imagine every word, phrase, pursed-lip sound,
curse, night scream condensed to different liquids.
I feel awash, immersed in pools, oceans of words
floundering, gasping, thrashing, drowning in
what I have said, spoken, yelled and sworn.
Bays, gulfs, fjords of everything ever uttered
gush over me in a tidal wave of remorse.

Light words, flippant words with lack of
substance. Consonants hollowed like b's, p's,
vowels buoy. Gasoline balloons to the surface
water skins of swirled membrane rainbows.
Look-good-words, polite words with razorbacks,
Trojan Horse kind of phrases complete with whiney.
Boil off silently words, clouding explosive words
invisibly, waiting to ignite and rage down a marriage,
trigger a war, make fun of a young McDonald's
employee who has just dropped a tray of trash.

Medium dense words shelved, stacked in bars
Ego, arrogant like cooling effect, first drink skin chill.
Stomach, heart and head extremes so you can
experience Arctic on the outside, inside hell.
So miscible mixing with life and fears, tear
pools so deep, heartache has thermoclines.
Deeper, darker, demons, divorce layered
like a slumping wedding cake slathered
with arsenic frosting and hemlock honey.

Lead heavy words sink & hold my attention,
glistening, reflecting toxic truths like mercury.
Thoughts so ferric, no matter how you tear
them apart they align and attract magnetically.

Cyclonic words circle like an emotional wagon
train where the wagons in front and back are
yesterday and tomorrow's straight-jacket.
My arms strapped to my side by time and fate.

Gasp, overlooking Montana's Missouri. My liquid
words gurgle and choke in past sound drowned.

Junked

Ever smelled of your own rust like
your life has been scrapped, junked?
Precision machinery of youth, middle-age
gears frozen, jammed, no one to repair you.
Grit packed even in the sexual gearbox.

Smell of iron, ochre, overheated oil like
all glands, gonads have been spent—
pheromones, hormones, and orgasms expended.
Nothing but evaporating rainbow glimmers
gasoline prismatic stripes floating on water.

Radiator thoughts and dreams cool the high-speed
engine of life. Drips ooze antifreeze leaks.
All passions, great thoughts maybe now poison,
waiting for some unsuspecting animal, attracted
by the sweet taste of poetic but lethal words.

Always liked junkyards—progress's scrap heap.
Chaos of past consumption in great clutter mounds.
Many ways to interpret useful, what wasn't.
All the odd parts juxtaposed with new understandings,
created yet another kind of machine—memory.

The Gaming Fields

Six airplane miles below irrigated circles of corn, wheat,
become autumn gold and bronze coins, covering harvest
odds on the eastern Montana irrigated prairie game board.

Bets sit waiting for the dice of season and weather to roll—
winners or wreak havoc. Sense game board of land played
out, irrigated casino chips ready to blow away like tumbleweeds.

Pretend to play generational eat or not eat roulette here.
Bet on black for land productivity for my children and red
on grandchildren—at least one generation won't starve.

Wheel spins, balls fly away with eroded soil, gold coins
disintegrate and melt into gray dust. Stacked deck-rigged
wheel. Gamble the West's future—house of loss always wins.

Locked Out of Me

I think I have locked me out of me.
As a Havre child I felt everything.
The "Hey, hey fatty two-by-four,"
"Bookworm," "Little arty farty."
Word knives twisted in my gut.
First door closed—I ignored names.

Skippy, my dog, got hit in the street.
Crawled nineteen steps up the porch,
died in my arms, while I prayed and pleaded
to a vengeful god for forgiveness. Surely
I had done something wrong. I closed the
door between me and my god. God left.

Then years of head filling numbing education,
engineering formulas, day-to-day reality
pushed into corner realms of abstract.
Added a return-on-investment, make-believe
wife—pollination, multiplication—last division.
American Dream morphed to a Hydra.

Stayed padlocked in my head. Never felt
pain—whiskey/gin whipped the hurt into tiny
spaces the size of 22 cartridges. Fired them at
friends, associates and family. Used smoke,
shock waves to keep everyone ducking for shelter.
Bank accounts, portfolio increased—soul to zero.

Been fiddling lately with the old combination lock.
One click back to 1965, feel air blowing through
Pipestone Pass hair as I rode my Triumph bike
home. Overpowered by the simple love for my
parents, imagining them in their daily rhythms.

Twist forward to today. Tumblers click—but,
though improving slightly, still locked out of me.

Centerpieces of Blindness

Children have become central like suns,
huge adorable stars that we now revolve around.
Drag, weight, spin of our genes makes me wobble.
Our lives not even planets anymore, only asteroid belts,
slowly drawn in and consumed in offspring coronas.

Vices, ah, gambling that vacuums away money, frenzied
I'll-pay-you-back tomorrows while hawking heirlooms,
selling plasma, juggling VISA card balances like live
grenades, groveling for under cushion change and kid's
lunch money—even asking an only son to sell a kidney.

Work, the numbers, proposals, even poem deadlines
enslave. Type O blood, universal donor of energy, ideas,
inventions that infest, become terminal parasites.
Type-A behavior, grades recorded for everything,
except the degree and speed of my declines.

Ah, love. I am the best "good" person for her absolutely—
after the 2-3 other best persons resigned in terror
because I shared, touched, loved, and respected
women to the point where divorce decrees were
cheaper than domestic assault and restraining orders.

Excellent night, peripheral and 20/20 vision.
Centerpieces hide deep in our blindness.

Small Town Check-Up

Checked out Belcherville, TX, trash-weed
embedded, plastic bags shredded by wind & sand
like a reputation torn with foul words, cleaver lies.
Beer cans, Burma Shave signs, old storefronts
sprouting fractured broken glass & deflated dreams,
Red River in the distance—memories of the dead West.

Glasgow, MT. Air Force left the base three decades ago.
Only thing landing & taking off are tumbleweeds.
Base a ghost town, Glasgow town drying up so fast
citizens turned to walking jerky or mummies. Mute
lips utter silent words that always end in leave, gone, bye,
lost, and dead. Can't be heard by anyone. All died or left.

Vici, OK, near the Oklahoma panhandle,
the only life being drawn from two miles down.
Brine 200 million year old seawater with a pinch
of iodine that drives the town economy. So poor
potholed streets where ramshackle buildings lean
on each other like dying soldiers after battle.

Blue River, OR, a former gold and old growth timber
town, plus the new Cougar Dam reservoir in the 1930s.
Last café closed, liquor store gone, acres of old mill
barracks burned & bankrupted. Local school,
Highway 126 skirts past the town like
a jugular artery completely bypassing the brain.

Small rural-town diagnosis—terminal.

Bar-Coded Life

The sun is hung low hammocked in the coming winter south,
felling great slabs of Ponderosa Pine shadows and light across the
        highway
like thousands of piano keys becoming a Cascade highway bar-
code strip
I scan along at 65 mph, picking up signals from the asphalt, the
        mountains,
steering a grocery cart of feelings, heart and memory laser
        scanning each,
to value them, add up the costs of life today, so I know what I
        owe.
I think of my daughter, who worked as a grocery checker last
        summer,
scanning the stuffing habits of regular, hurting crippled hearts
        from Tacoma:

    The tampons, feminine hygiene products, *National
    Enquirer*
    celebrating no pregnancy this month yet pleading for any
    intimacy.

    Wine, beer, cigarettes injected one way or another to
    deaden the
    fears, quiet the loneliness, and let us dig the grave for our
    dreams again today.

    The long on image foods stuffed with fat and
    carbohydrates,
    as if we were trying to glue up every tear duct escape to the
    outside world.

The products of my life are bar-coded, registered and tallied:
lost marriage, missing-in-action behind-friendly-lines for my
      children,
debts to lovers, debts to the ideas that have given me mental
      breath.
I drive only several miles, the car zebra-ing through the
      shadow strips.
But I have scanned my life, the cost of what I bought, and like
any consumer, much of what I bought I didn't need or want.
The treetops tickle the fall sunlight and
my tires keep scanning the shadows,
I feel now as settled as any shadowy thing can.

Dying Is an Art Form

Dying to an alcoholic is a 3-D flesh/gene art form.
I—Gaugin/Monet. The liquid palette of my trade—
Finlandia Cranberry, Merlot and Burgundy for reds,
Chardonnays and Harpers for tans and gold,
Blue Curacao, Sapphire Gin, then Midori Green,
Black Death vodka with sweet licorice for ink lines.
Vodka in volume—fastest drying and crying solvent.

Brush-stroked each day sunset bruises, blurred pointillism
visions complete with July 4th firework glory bursts.
During night, imagined masterpieces turn simplistic,
shaded, smudged. Frames black, dark crimson
fears, Edvard Munch screams and clots of quick dying.
Painted in my head while ass glued to barstools, aisle
airline seats—to get to the peeing, booze, and dying faster.

Imagined sculpting as well—granite chips flying, my
version of Michelangelo's David emerging in Florence
to raving Italian acclaim. Chisel dust revealed my
masterpiece—granite arm, wine glass moving to a head
of perpetually puckered lips, all perched on a rock barstool.

Dreamed of creating an Ibsen or Einstein bust. All I chiseled
were images of me fear-eyed, trapped, grasping, clawing,
never smashing out of the granite bottle of my addiction.

Got a new frame, palate and set of chisels. Sculpt, paint,
even write. Emerge, limb-by-limb, from the perpetually
black nightmare frame of night and block of drunk.

Crowded into the Margins

Felt, lived, dreamed my youth, non-ending exuberant,
boundless energy, economic growth with double-
digit hope. Lived like a Pony Express rider—rode
every opportunity mount to a hot-lather sweat exhaustion.
Pervasive education oozed from multi-degreed pores,
a whole generation closeting pieces of our past away.
All had words, most had jobs, some had fantastic thoughts.
Vowels & sentences, protests, poetry howls, press
releases, front-page pictures, and GI Bill. Constitution
became life, bait to draw out the freedom lovers—gays,
women, black, and handicapped. Everyone finally included in
the Yellow Pages of the country illustrated in color.
But rainbow Polaroid prints turned out to be blank,
smudges of blacks, barcodes for jails to keep things
in racial place. Religious freedom went from
Neopolitan-to-artificial Costco vanilla. Hispanic,
Asian, Native American progress written in disappearing
ink, citizens hidden yet again in the country's footnotes.
The middle class, once the gut beginning, middle, end,
now an inflamed appendix. Table of contents of country
taken over by super rich, GNP, politics, oil, annual reports,
mergers, down-sizings. All relegated to democracy hinterlands.
The People crowded into the margins of their own country.

288 Months Pregnant

Been pregnant 288 months with this innovative idea.

Three or four rounds of financial investment fathers,
my body used like a marshaling yard for a D-Day
victory invasion one day, the next day a tail-between-
my-legs retreat worse than Napoleon leaving Russia.
Been on the front line so long, my head has grown
a helmet. I dig a trench even when I go to the movies.

Every four years politics intervenes. Oil embargos,
9/11, wars, changes in Fortune 500 partner management,
no money, some money, foreign grants, strong board,
weak partners, intellectual property pirates & thieves.
Desert Storm, new alliances in Iceland, South Africa
musical chairs around oil. Then Afghanistan and Iraq.

Worried sick about venture stillbirth, a breach.
Can't push the last yards through the start-up birth canal,
then infanticide concerns if it is a healthy birth. Yeah,
some want this infant dead. No one likes a bastard,
green, renewable heir to the black cartel oil throne.
Long time to make oil—longer to replace even a part.

Need a specialized kind of Lamaze for our young
engineers, who internalize pressures in their hearts,
joints. Heads whirl with negatives as though oil
company equations could predict their failure.
Need soft touches, heavy panting & loving breathing,
warm Kevlar swaddling. They have iron alloy parents.

Maybe this year water will break, contractions start.
288 months and counting for an idea to maybe get born.

Aroga Moth

Plush. Oregon isn't plush, except for sagebrush.
High desert sage gray-green whorled with knotted
stems, fibers woven to Indian moccasins.
Leaves are natural de-wormers for sheep, antelope,
pungent scent rubbed between fingers, patted
on cheeks—mountain man aftershave. Sage an
insect incubator and emergency winter deer feed.

Aroga moth was introduced in the 1960's, wiped
out sage for miles. Crested wheat grass planted.
Excuse some say to get rid of sage once and for all.
Plant a better forage crop for cattle and sheep.
Short tufted, waves stiffly in fall breeze,
blonde, nape of the neck, seductive until
you see history versus hype side by side.

Busted. Fooled again in the Oregon outback by
supposed biological experts, agencies responsible for the
common good—of a very few. Aroga Moth
ate the sage and then any wisdom remaining.

Frantic in the Rubble

I have this recurring dream of a bright shining new morning
until I walk outside the house. Everything within sight
      leveled—
London 1940 WWII blitz—rubble heaps taller than buildings.

Every misshapen concrete chunk, every splintered wooden stud
imprinted with names of friends cheated, promises un-kept, and
      love trashed.
All documented in dried blood, ash, and body char. I am the
      smoking gun.

I see my ex-wife standing in the rubble some distance away—
      smiling.
Head wrapped in paper bandages—written abuse scrawled on
      the backside
of the divorce decree, waving alimony checks the size of
      American flags.

Broken pictures of my children, pieces of their favorite toys
      everywhere
like we had just completed a weekend of play and were tidying
      up—
decapitated dolls, smashed computer games, and burned kid
      books.

Everything seems raw inside me, pained, unplugged, and
      pulped,
as though all my vital organs have been playing musical chairs,
extracted one by one until nothing's left but bloodstains on a
      lone stool.

Past surely wasn't this bad? But family portraits are on
      concrete slabs,
radiation shadows. Not just nuclear bombs for Hiroshima,

Nagasaki. I
nuked them daily, weekly—family dying of radiation exposure
to me.

Frantic in the rubble until tonight, when the dream comes
again.

The Undefeated Gunslinger

Seven-foot double-wide liquor cabinet,
cowboy hat sitting on top,
a massive no-head gunslinger.

Swing-glass doors open like a vest
lit from within so the drinker
doesn't have to fumble in the dark.

Stand across the room hands at my side.
Fingers twitch, throat parched.
Face to face. One shot will kill me.

I turn and walk away. Today.

Diesel Fumed Home

I sit at the end of Central Avenue, Kearney, Nebraska.
Watch grain and coal unit trains Doppler-throb past,
smell that diesel fuel, creosote, rich-oily track stench.
Memories shake, vibrate back to Montana Hi-Line rails.
Thoughts, feelings pulse, roar through me over steel
laid down in my child head forty years ago.
The smell of my father's railroad clothes. From that
diesel closeness, I knew what a man smelled like.
Remember the ulcer that ate him from the inside
out as trips swung him, rumbled back, throbbed forth.
My father a piece of meat dangled between Havre and
            Whitefish.
The railroad digesting him year after year. I see my
brother daily switching and mounting big toy engines,
dealing out his living-day cards. A second generation on the
Santa Fe-Burlington Northern. My father is buried,
every track serves as a living ribbon monument.
I want my brother remembered as well by this poem.
Diesel fumed home.

Hero Buried on Page Seven

He wasn't a political leader we know—
      another front-page administration deception,
      shadow government led by Darth Vader look-alikes,
      Hollywood, Senate generating wars as fast as possible.
      Real US storm troopers hunt peasants & children.

He wasn't in entertainment or sports—
      Brett Favre's football comeback yet again,
      another "star" failing Betty Ford rehab.
      Beautiful Mind nominated for best picture,
      none of the actors even understand algebra.

He wasn't in business—
      newspapers yapping up quarterly profits and sales,
      out-sourced local bar-code laser scanning outfit
      (serving Walmart, Safeway) to China. 120 jobs gone,
      cut health benefits; management bonuses up 100%.

He was just a page seven obituary by-line—
      He was maybe not a hero, maybe just lived
      a life—no deceptions, lies, no Hail Marys,
      not firing his friend and neighbor, working,
      living, being just the person he was.

We need people to look up to.
I am starting to look for them on page seven.

The Borax Chubb

The Steens drew me in October to Eastern Oregon.
Alford Desert floor, gazing, up wishing Steens harsh
cliffs were adoring parents instead of decades of
all-seeing escarpment memories. Space absorbs.
Distance masks maps with dusty dirt roads.

Finally telltale hot spring steam roiling amidst frigid
sage. Geothermal creek no more than a block long,
foot wide, six inches deep cooling as it flows before
it's sponged into the Alford sand. Algae red rust to
ruby. 20 Mule Team Borax smell, foul sulfur whiffs.

Parts per million arsenic and boron. So high it's toxic.
Nothing ordinary could live here except the Borax Chubb.
An inch and a half long minnow, evolutionary anomaly not
found in Yellowstone or Iceland. Borax Chubb survives
against all odds. I can survive outside Montana.

I Think I Will Follow Her Lead

At first it was coffee. Fresh roasted, ground
beans from Eugene. Allan Brothers, Wandering Goat,
custom Orsini and Lille. Took my MJB, Folgers, and Yuban,
shelved them permanently between peat & sawdust.

Then it was Bed & Breakfast. At first I scoffed.
Bozeman Continental Inn $39, Motel 6 perfect,
maybe Hampton Inn splurge—engineer in me.
Graduated to: Howlers Inn in Montana—a B&B
wolf sanctuary, complete with bottle-feeding cubs,
ranch guesthouse in the Oregon Steens,
complete with real mule deer on the lawn.
Gone from saddle and blanket on the ground to
queen beds and all I had to do was pull back
my attitude and get under the comforter with Susan.

Organic Food? Laughed at first. My scientific
knee-jerk rebuttals—only nitrogen, phosphorus,
carbon dioxide at my contempt-prior-to-investigation
fingertips. But she reminded me that breast cancer is
linked to insecticides. Try arguing with a woman
who's been through chemo. She adds, "Don't get me
started on genetically-modified crops or Round-Up
resistant soy or increasing arsenic in the city reservoirs."
I didn't want to admit it. All these chemicals
compliments of us chemistry folks. True—toxic.

Now farmers market shopper, organic green,
eat less thinking of ways to compost, recycle.
It's been a long day, writing longhand, waiting for
winter storms to pass, and electric power to return.
She suggests, candle in hand, we go to bed early.
I think I will follow her lead yet again.

Gift of an Adopted Chester

Chester has a long blond mane, equine tail flows.
He usually is led by his donkey friend, Babs.
Chester directed by nudges, smells to safe ground
following Babs, who leaves a bray sound trail,
coaxing invitation and stumble-free assurances.

It wasn't mentioned was it? Chester is blind.
Retinas detached, he can only see bleary shadows,
light and dark smears, like Plato's cave.
Good and evil? To Chester evil has a decidedly
human form. Chester's sight remembered
before shadows were male fists, chunks of jaw-
breaking wood, heavy blows taking away any
joy Chester gave to his former mistress. A wife
abuser turned to easier target animal abusing.
No pony 911s. Chester was rescued in Sultan, WA.

Tuesday, there was freezing McKenzie River
rain, so cold my joints and jaws seem to pain.
Fog, mist hung low over the dark water, background black, tints of deep blue, and gray splotches.
Felt darkness inside the day swing down from
Eagle Rock and crash into the house, leveling
any positive mood. Opened the mail, found Chester,
one-eyeing me, peeking through dishwater blond
mane. We are Chester's new adopted parents,
donation Xmas gift from my son, Sean. Chester,
Babs, the river, the dark and yet a sudden
great brightness from a trail of compassion.

Chirping Lake

Visiting LA daughter bundled, two coats, scarf,
red beanie. Two days before Halloween at 9000
feet on the Steens escarpment. Walk into Pine Lake—
crystalline cold around us, chills between us.
We the actors on this frigid stage have no lines.
Seemingly ice-berged into gone-a-long-time mime.
Powdered snow skitters on the ice—cataract colored.
Lake surrounded with aspen white, black stripes.
Mud on the beach edge puffed, frozen, expanded.
Pop-corned dirt. Walk is a cross between crunch and crinkle.
I underhand, rocket-up a big pebble. Apogees, falls
gha-thunk as it penetrates the thin ice tympanum.
Ice acts like a drum—whole lake surface recoils a bit,
sucks in air through the hole. White clusters of bubbles
jostle like children standing at a window. Bubbles
peer up. A gurgle escapes through the puncture.
"Wow, this lake talks!" she whispers. She skips a
first, found flat rock. A chirp? We look around for
birds, flying, in trees—none. More rock experimenting,
skipping at intervals. More chirps. One after another
bouncing tweeting, bringing spring sounds to winter.
We mimic songbirds with smooth pebbles.
Bounce odd music up into the snowy Steens.
Daughter bundled two coats, scarf, red
beanie. She is smiling, engaged. Gha-thunk,
chirp, we warm, play back into each others' lives.
I skip, soar, I flap my wings being near her again.

Bunkhouse Love

We turn off the space heaters at night.
Dry starlight chilled high desert air
sucks the heat from the room
in several giant post-midnight gasps.

We lie piled high with blankets
recuperating from each other's absence,
my reverses of business, ideas in hairpins knots,
her teaching images colliding with reality.

The mule deer have been company,
black eyes bounding over fences,
blending into the gray-green of sage color
in our bunkhouse planet lit front yard.

Farm chickens, white turkeys,
peacocks complete with NBC advertising
rival the quail as they brisk around
trailing us hoping we are crumbling.

Someone needs to start the space heater
in the early morning of us reconnecting,
take the edge off the chilled night
of this gone-too-long relationship.

Instructions on the Inside

I am adrift like a bottle afloat in the North Sea.
Carry encrypted messages, ink bleeding slightly,
folded and crumpled, like engineering blueprints.
Reams of secrets and codes hidden in the up, down buoy.
There should be armed guards—even motion detectors.
Topographical-lay of the land of me is a corked fifth.

I am so out of touch with me, but I can't crack open
myself to read what I may have written. Undiagnosed
talent, basic professional amnesia. A voyeur, I only
peer through chrome-green wine bottle glass, see
distorted instructions for operating my life. I am
ocean adrift with garbled messages and lonely nights.

I am the only quasi-thinking machine, bio-vessel
I know where my own operating instructions are
trapped on the inside, Kanji characters written in lemon
juice—only appear with heat, and I can't read. Am
alien in my own body most time and the last to know
me or the alien within. All I can do is grab the bottle.

The Gap

The evidence of everything we are or aren't,
all the forensics to condemn us for life, or
free us for eternity is in the gap.

Gap between the growing eggplant colored bruise
on a woman's back and abuser's belief that stress
was caused by her and she deserved hammering.

Gap between the retina & craving brain
where seeing the needle go in the arm
equates to heroin pleasure, not overdose death.

Gap between 9/11 terrorist activities, paranoia to open
anthrax spore mail, and playing into the hands of media.
Slight of hand hiding lucrative oil pipelines across
        Afghanistan.

Gap between the Enron executive rhetoric
not knowing details, "no one informed me,"
new brand of Hitler. Like Goering, Speer, SS.

Gap between you and me that disappears
when we are together, widens like the Grand Canyon
when apart. Bridged by trust, built of thinnest string,

written words, poetic lines, old-fashioned letter
paragraphs dropped like sandbags between us
as we try to flood over the gap into each other.

Natural Falling Bodies

Wind howls, old growth forest limbs crack,
make hundred-fifty-foot falls whumping the roof
with branches thick as thighs, amputated limbs
twitch, but bleed and sap coagulate out of sight.

Thuds, cracks happen—storm artillery bursts.
Pine cones grenade down as though paratroopers
dropped unto the canopy and skirmish down trunks.
Forest floor littered with wounded, biomass deserters.

Needles silent stiletto slivers, ever sifting.
Green moss string segments stretched, sprung,
little avalanches of stick twigs and raining,
knocked down, split by a bowling ball sun

that rolled nothing at ten pin needles, but a ray.
Wind flutters that merely suggests a topple,
panic ensues like a stock market crash.
Needles wind-jettisoned and fall like lemmings.

My body cartilage is lumping at the joints.
Vertebrae compressed, squeezed, and no rebound.
Spine collapsing, body thickening, and puddling.
Hair migrating to lower altitudes, hairlines higher,

sentences getting compressed like shrunken heads.
Syllables sliced, fall off the table from the keyboard.
Other examples of naturally falling bodies
in an old growth McKenzie River forest.

Departure of Parts

My hands hold an open book and are growing
farther away from my body. Eyes see at greater
distances as though future is more important than present,
but I might be looking in the wrong direction.

Ears not as universally perceptive but selective,
screening out advertisements, seeming trivia,
like your question asking what I want to
do with the rest of my life and how about supper.

Used to enjoy smelling and sniffing everything.
A day was like being in a multi-car crash of a
winged florist, perfume maker, fresh-baked bread,
sweet benzene gasoline & Joe's septic tank services.

Now I am selective, remote like my nose
is Pinocchio after a lie, ten feet out in front
where I am sniffing for traces, hints of you,
not Fendi, Ambush, Obsession, just the raw you.

When I touch you, I feel away, as if I have gone
on a trip to Mars, reach back and no matter how
far I stretch into memory, I have to live with these
departure of your parts.

Road Kill Past

Morning steeped in shaking gold, crimson skies.
Yellowstone blue liquid sapphires, caret sparkle,
new pitch-black asphalt scissors, and dotted-line
cuts up the valley into carcasses of space.

Road is washed ahead in blood, a
deer life coagulated into the asphalt,
thin filmed hemoglobin red rusting.
Speed intersected one night and a life.

We have been in each other's lives
for so long it's before, beyond memory.
I want to hang in and salvage crumbs of past
that took years to make a day together.

This past relationship hid in the night,
created by decades of single days,
false expectations then headlight highlighted,
impact sudden and a death quick.

Thin film of love laying out there,
covering so much of us yet so little.
Red heartache left with sapphires and gold.
Fear, love and beauty become future road kill.

Heart in Exile

Since leaving Montana after 1967 college,
my heart has been in economic induced exile.
I have been pumped dry. All creative thoughts
depleted like Sunburst and Shelby oilfields.
Paid handsomely to look past and discount my own life.

Hemorrhaged inventions to other moneyed realms,
developed business, plants, jobs in places
like Japan, China, Iceland and Oklahoma.
My waning blood pipeline of innovation
buried alive, deep beneath foreign soil.

Montana thoughts like red blood cells, however,
circle, circle inside like vultures hunting the past.
Finally drag out Raggedy-Ann words into piecemeal
poems trying to portray picture perfect mule deer,
more than likely ends describing flattened road kill.

Memories become teepee poles of new thought.
Each car visit, Horizon flight back, back steals string of
words and hordes of hijacked images. Miles and space
wigwam me off the Montana extinction list. Heart
exile becomes a kind of belated coming home party.

What Day?

I have been looking back over my past,
trying to figure out what day started what.

The day I started the nuclear research job at 23,
or the day in youth I created my first stink
bomb, exploded rocket fuel, or pressed rose
petal fragrances into lard that my mother reluctantly
applied to her hands—my homemade Oil of Olay.

What day did I become a father?
Moment of conception of my first son,
or birth of the fourth or was it that idea at 18
that my children, if any, might be the first
generation ever to be college educated?

What day did I become a good lover to you?
The first time, last time, multi-orgasm time?
Or was it the time I started to make up,
tell little stories whispered in your ear while
rest of your body listened to more basic calls?

What day did I start writing, not engineering,
business plans, memos—but the poetry & novels?
Five years ago—seven? Or was it sitting
4th floor Culbertson Hall Bozeman, MT in 1965,
thinking, *Who said I couldn't be both a writer & scientist?*

Here I am with all these gifts & trails
but no footprints to lead back to the source,
no cards about who, when the present was sent.
Not a clue how any of this started.

But 12 March 2012 when I wrote this was the day,
I started thinking gratefully about starting days.

Simple Subtraction

1971 minus 1905 equals 66—simple subtraction.
His gravestone lays flat like a doormat
blue-collar railroaders could easily identify.
All it says is *Arthur C. Father 1905-1971*;
it doesn't say felled by kidney infection,
      two minus one equals pain,
      one minus one equals death.
It doesn't say lost to an ulcerated stomach,
      eaten away by a conductor's job,
      worrying about too many freight trains.

1973 minus 1917 equals 56—simple subtraction.
Her gravestone lays flat in a grassy patch of cemetery road,
the cover of a big granite book never opened by anyone.
All it says is *Val, Mother 1917-1973*.
It doesn't say a word about her lost dreams,
      sons gone to other women's arms,
      her own lovers dead.
It doesn't explain any part of the reason so much had
      flown from her life, a self-directed bullet, the
      only way to stop last thoughts from leaving.

Simple subtraction doesn't explain any of the losses
or why they are buried on opposite
sides of the same cemetery.

Peacefully Died

It is a blessing loved ones tout and proclaim
that he or she died peacefully in sleep.

When I sleep, I swirl in riptides,
swim with exploding depth charges.
Giant clanking shipwrecks of ideas
grind, cut each other in half. Some
vessels sink instantly, some linger
to watch all passengers drown first.

Nothing but serial slow-motion escapes
from high-speed monsters with rotating
chainsaw jaws going through femurs
like they were blades of spring grass.
Saw my love with breasts yanked
from chest walls, dipped in black cancer,
radiated and chemo scar tissue welded back on.

My brother still wades though VC rice
paddies, cuts off leeches, digs out
embedded shrapnel, and takes wounded Marines
"lost" for a two-week stroll behind enemy lines.
Every other night, I fend off bottles of 140
proof thrown like internal Molotov cocktails.
Singes a few vital organs, cooks my liver,
blinds me and corkscrew eviscerates me.
Then the dreams get down right really ugly.

Obviously whoever lipped this cliché
has never dreamed at least the way I dream.
Die in peace in restful sleep—my ass.

SUM OF ALL GIVEAWAYS

Gave away those childhood years in Montana, railroad spiking,
baling hay, rock quarrying, experimenting with explosives,
practicing lines for *Crucible* & *Midsummer's Night Dream,*
Importance of Being Ernest, tinkering to undo bra clasps,
studying engineering & philosophy until I was an amalgam of
rugged mountains, wide intellectual plains & cloudy idealism.

Gave away my mid-twenties, thirties to unbridled married life.
Each child giving me an extra heart chamber so now I have
two hearts—mine and an extra made of son ventricles and
daughter/son auricles. Force-fed an MBA. Promptly Fortune
500 eaten. Dealt with borderline criminal technical ideas,
government programs, boondoggles that rival fake NASA
        flights to the moon.

Gave away forties, fifties to my own impassioned ideas
of replacing oil-based chemicals with sugar, making Iceland
a center of no oil, no gas, separating every chemical made
instead of wasting molecules that can never be made again.
Nearly died, came back from dead, crawled out of Purgatory
divorce, disease, partners dying & recovering from cancer.

Gave away more than years—dam bursts of affections,
flared sexual energy. Met a handful of women that saved,
loved and purposed me. Each love like a duel between
blowtorches and dry ice. We either smelted each other to gold
nuggets or froze us in some state of suspended animation.
Each love a rope to the future and a noose hanging the past.

I might have been lessened by the sum of all that I gave away.
Big pieces of me are spore on the Kruger Park veld,
skin moss-draped over Reykenes Peninsula jagged lava, and
arm bones stuck out of the Bears Paw Mountains, waving.

But I have all these points of me plastered to a sticky note past of flagging memories. I am the sum of all my giveaways.

Working Up to Common

Came in unique, self-imagined Renaissance
man—engineer, businessman, scientist, hybrid
Montana mountain-man and da Vinci.
International, hell, even galactic traveler
on and off the barstool. Just couldn't
stop drinking. Put it down often,
but couldn't put it down for very long.
Stress you know? Damn strain! Poor me?

Came in a genius, high IQ, educated
definitely beyond my intellectual capacity,
but couldn't figure out that alcohol,
not a deadly virus, bacteria, mold, but
FDA approved, regulated, brainless
saccharomyces yeast was pushing ethanol
into bottles, cans, fifths that strangled my life.

Came in and no one understood me.
Had to self-medicate with booze to get
through the day without "'cide effects"—
suicide, homicide, genocide. Needed alcohol
for the ever shorter, fleeting moments of soap-
bubble peace in an angry porcupine world.

All the intellect, prejudice, intelligence, ego
turned out to be allies, agents, spies of the disease.
Terrible thing to find out and accept the prized
possessions of self were enemies inside me.

Slowly working from mad genius up to solid common.

Simple Wants

All I wanted was a damp autumn Havre basement smell
with whiffs of iodine & cinnamon, sulfur lingering,
miracles bibled on every chemistry textbook page,
wicking suck sounds of an alcohol burner, test tube boiling.
Didn't fathom I'd build plants operating at pressures
of Jupiter, incarcerating hydrogen in thick steel vessels—
equivalent of squeezing a Hindenburg dirigible into a beer can.

Wanted a simple Thoreau cottage, cot, books.
Sunburned gandy-dancer railroad pick and shovel days
Perfect. Sweat airing out the inside of muscles
in a delicate balance—idealism, drive and peace of mind.
Didn't really want corporate rat-race-ugly, laced
with oozing radioactive wastes in the Columbia
from our own nuclear weapons program, nerve gas
just another desert crop in Umatilla, Oregon, and phenol-
poisoned drinking water that Thalidomides whole towns.

Wanted blocks of time to invent, glean obscure words
& mysteries hidden in books, microscope slides, data.

Ended up prying minutes away from schedules like
barnacles hacked from the boat bottom of a business day.
Dealt with scabs of time at airports, 4 a.m. wake-ups,
weekend bacon-thin slabs of time stolen from family.
Wrote. Ignored festering financial and business wounds.

Ended up technically becoming expert in separations. Am
able to strip baby molecules away from their close twins,
mothers, extract thyroid bound iodine from miles beneath
Oklahoma, make turpentine into perfumes, and use Arctic krill
oil to make Shiseido lipstick.

Simple wants have become more complex.

Mustang Love

Like a wild stallion and an
unbridled free spirited mare,
we mustang trample around in love,
High Country, Big Sky living.

You fear saddles, being cinched in,
being ridden anymore by past mistakes,
expectations that cornered you in box canyons.
Daughter fillies tug heavy on your heart.

I resist the halter, ego-sharpened spurs,
living a life run by corporate masters
headed for a kind of soul slaughter, ending
up retired—euphemism for wild horse dog food.

Both of us hate being iron-shoe shod,
so we can't leave our hoof prints,
our words, naturally where they should lie,
nestled in poems, books, long-range thoughts.

Fields Station Café

Founded 1881, serving food, gossip,
deaths, births for over a century,
so many voices stored in booths
they stacked them as the Steens.
Senate of Harney County—first three
through the gas station/café door.
House convenes every Saturday night,
Lincoln Monument in the corner,
drinking coffee in a cloud of smoke.
Smithsonian is the knickknack mart,
hunting gear interspersed with Fritos,
Quaker State, Pepsi, and 30-06 shells.
Ice cream chilling next to a locked liquor cabinet.
Memorabilia from WWII, Korea.
Local jail where lives get strapped
to stools, gambling trips to Winnemucca,
taking the social security checks
on a one-way binge, no change return trip.
4818 hamburgers and fries served in 2002
January to October 28th, 5685 milkshakes,
their own billions & billions served.
Outdoor zoo, doe grazing edge of town
eyeing the mutt pacing in the pick-up bed.
America in a store. A country of five people.

My Paloose Son Sleeps

It's mid October, just rained, black, the final headlight stab before
light, those Paloose dawn moments when black night and wet soil
sleep together in wheat straw gold and crimson dawn streaks.
A blanket fold tucks my sleeping son, dormitory perched a
sleeping falcon. His dreams of history and psychology rimming
around like a high school basketball shot that will never fall.

Pine trees seem to be running in the dark to hide in the gullies.
Some are caught and frozen in their tracks by the light.
They stand shake and gasp thinking they have hid from
my sight. Young male hormones course beneath taught skin,
beard and sideburns and that short crew cut stubble caught
growing in the night. Fear of loneliness and what I am
becoming cause a kind of trembling that I can only sense.

New dawn bounces in from the East off the clouds, mountains,
up and down Clearwater. Green and red orange
splashes of color like Roman candles around every curve.
A new man grows with all these thoughts careening in that young
magnificent mind. A sleep stew where the future decants,
separating the past. Magical dawn—priceless son.

Gold Code of Montana

August "wheat is elevator-ed"—harvest is in on the Hi-Line.
Gold durum kernels litter the ground around grain silos—
Hansel and Gretel leaving a trail for next spring. Bushels
carry ancient messages of renewability, seeds a photosynthetic
cassette ready to silently replay the past again and again.

Auric scented leaves fall in the Missouri breaks,
parachutes of gold glide, slip-slide onto riverbanks like
Army airborne taking the low ground before winter.
Slowly soft touch surfaces yield to gold-leaf crystal crunch.
Names of each day color reported in the fall book of 2008.

The banks of the Madison, Jefferson and Gallatin
get ready for the Loomis trucks of fall gold to be deposited.
Smoothed wet stones play rainbow catch with the sunset.
Trout gargle with the light and spit out silver nuggets, and
gold flecks hit my arteries and plaque up my smiling heart.

It's not the luster that ransacks my eyes to hoard.
It's not the glint that sets off pangs of greed.
It's the gold code of Montana that soars my soul.

Tambourine Day

Late October, the freeze has come to the Steens.
Quaking Aspen, either plated gold or tarnished
silver black hang from zebra limbs and striped
rumped trunks. Snow staying through the day on
gorge north slopes, claiming half of the Little
Blitzen, Kiger, Big Indian, like an unwanted
homesteading invading enemy. The gold leaves
whistle and the black foliage hums a sound. A
cross of crackling dry paper and buzzing beehive.
The stilled night mountain moves in morning—
breezed purrs. Thistles snow-coated shake, shimmy,
strip in front of you. Pond ice—window clear,
brittling on the shallow lakes—melts. Oreo-cookied
roads thaw, leaving no white filling only black.
Quaking leaf tambourines play, setting a day
harmony, as though winter and summer had
declared a truce to record a perfect rustling moment.

16 People Today

My daughter, Holly, and I did a late October car cruise.
Started at B&B in Diamond population eight. Plan—
French Glen, the Steens loop north side up, south down.
The town of Fields for lunch, Alford Desert hot springs
soak. Then back north along the Steens base,
counterclockwise back to Diamond. Two-hundred miles.

In the hotel at French Glen, four men sip coffee and
flirt with the hostess with a short lap created by
a set of even shorter legs. Only eligible female
in a county the size of Massachusetts. One man
said, "It's a break from pruning trees in the rain."
But this is eastern Oregon. There is no rain, no trees.

On the Steens summit, General Electric employee
taking a 9500 foot high digital picture of himself—
background—Alford Desert, Idaho, even distant St. Louis.
Hoarfrost covered bush lower left corner, making him
seem tethered on the brink, suspended like an apparition.
Next frame ascent to heaven? We *are* so close after all.

Holly waived at John & Katarina our B&B guest mates
from Denmark. They'd said over dinner the previous
night, "We know all the bumps in our Jutland flatness."
Steens was their first climb, first precipice, first escarpment.

Grizzled gas station attendant at Fields Station Café
doubled as grocer, mechanic, mayor, OTC pharmacist,
past and present curator. One woman (triples as cook,
waitress, dishwasher) and four burger wolfing patrons.
Wall scored hamburgers sold that year: 5,432. Shakes: 3,860.
McDonald's billions vs. one customer here—an event.

At Alford Hot Springs, one gentleman joined us.

74

Silently soaked his old joints until soothed & limbered.
"Howdy. Have a nice day," sum total of words in an hour.
Too many Hereford and Angus cattle to count, maybe
sixty deer, coyote, mountain sheep, eagles, hawks,
sage in such variety, over such an expanse, rivals infinity.
Oh, yeah—waved at one man in a pick-up driving past.
Saw sixteen people today—met the whole world.

Railroad Track Guitar

Single pair of steel wires string up the Columbia Gorge,
sidetracks fan into a six string railroad track guitar.
Stonehenge replica Washington side of the river,
audience of one ready for a concert in the Gorge.

A westbound train like a long finger strums, then hums
colored containers, box cars, tanks visual lyrics.
Racks of cars, passenger-less, with phantom gas move west,
tons of China-bound corn aching to swell in someone's mouth.
Steel beams wait for a Portland place to get an erection.

An eastbound—big base vibrates up river against gravity,
timber raw with the pain of cut and coagulated sap drying,
boxcars of chardonnay, corks licking the rocking wine,
frozen fish blocks that serve as their own grave stones,
flatcars of forklifts, and acres of plywood book-thin as paper.

Each train a new song, each Union Pacific or Santa Fe
a new gig, every siding standing room only concert.
A third generation 'trained' in rock bedding and rail rolling.
Can't get the Montana ballast out of my gizzard. Parallel lines
and endless lengths of reverberating power hidden in me.

Last Great Grandfathers

Your father's paternal grandfather, Arthur,
so coordinated he could shoot and hit falling stars,
tie trout flies with one powerful hand,
wanted to be a surgeon, live in Montana.
Loved pine woods, spring water, duck hunting.
Closest he got to medicine was his own home.

Your father's paternal grandfather, Arthur,
died in 1971, respected senior railroad brakeman,
Burlington Northern rails strapped to his back,
railroad ties—a kind of Montana cross—
nailed to his Havre hands by the depression.
Kidney infection, ulcers—medicine killed him.

Your father's maternal grandfather, Dan,
a small Huntley ranch-hand handyman,
who after the war ran the Billings Nye family dairy,
at 50 graduated from college by equivalency,
took correspondence law, passed the Montana bar,
transformed career, life and never left Poly Drive.

Your father's maternal grandfather, Dan,
became Yellowstone County prosecutor,
stories of robbers, thieves, Big Sky Sodom & Gomorrah,
quoted Robert Service, a little right of Goldwater.
Loved his camper, kids, grand kids, Lake Pend Oreille.
Alzheimer's took his poetry, stories, and his gentleness.

These two helped me cast out anchors
that took a long time to hit bottom.
My soul has been fixed in Montana ever since—
my way of staying close, showing respect.
Two men remain keys to a safety deposit box of place.
They will make you feel home here in Montana from their

beyond even though you have not been born yet.

These two great grandfathers are with you,
cheering you on, laying the groundwork, and
quietly showing you around like a guest.
They thank you, encourage you for who you are,
the biological sum total reason they existed.
You are the flower, but they are two of your fallen petals.

Last Great Grandmothers

Todd, your paternal grandmother, Alvera,
came from a his, hers, ours hybrid Scandinavian clan
with one sister, three steps and four "half's."
Depression stories of a jar of pickles for Xmas
where a Havre home & a job were "having it all."
Uneducated, but so literate, she could quote Frost.

Holly, your paternal grandmother, Alvera,
raised two sons, kept a house so clean
light would scrap its shoes before shining in.
A church deacon, painter of houses for cash
owned most of the petunias in Hill County.
Her beauty stopped traffic; addiction stopped her.

Chad, your maternal grandmother, Nona,
born & raised & lived in a one block stretch
so close she & her two sisters breathed the same air.
She was a Big Heart from the Big Sky,
could knit anything from quilts & sweaters
not to mention a permanent place in your heart.

Sean, your maternal grandmother, Nona,
raised two beautiful daughters and a son,
buried a husband, daughter-in-law, grand-daughter.
Knitted generations together, remembers the dead,
holds court in Billings, presides over grand halls of past,
the only regal-in-her-own-way queen I have ever met.

Children: so both of your grandmothers
lived close to Havre-Billings Montana mid-line.
They are like two mountain ranges,
each distinct & majestic in their own ways.
Both mines of gems and trip-mines of danger.
Waiting for you to come into the past and visit.

Average Conversation with My Daughter

Conversations used to be behind invisible shields
like the Lucas Death Star. Behind my beer and gin
real fears like being caught or worse yet confronted.
Liver panted—drinking, dying, knowing it was booze.

No admissions. Daughter ever suspicious, watched
me. She chose to share but motes, paper veneer of her
university life, any boyfriends anonymously hidden
like old Oz behind curtains and "I haven't met anyone."

Any conversation was like the Millenium Falcon in
pursuit of Empire fighters dog-fighting through asteroid
belts. Every topic quickly shot down, good things flamed
out in meteor showers of bad feelings and bullet holes.

Then I got sober and we somehow thawed over a year.
One summer we decided father-daughter to Iceland.
Now non-stop day/night dialogue around her Hollywood
screenwriting life, ideas and places we have shared:

> Imagine the real Noah's Arc being found in Iceland,
> poking out of a glacier loaded with frozen aliens.
>
> *Zen and the Art of Motorcycle Maintenance*—
> imagined motion picture with Montana as the frame.
>
> *The Break-Up Girl* script written by my
> daughter coming together as a woman.
>
> Ghosts in Virginia City past hover in the present,
> Boot Hill vampires firing bullets of garlic.
>
> She has told me now all about my new son-in-law.
> Our combined critical mass humor gets Emmys.

Average conversation with my daughter now like watching a galaxy being born with happy explosions in my head.

Passing Shadows

A quaking aspen tree shakes in the breeze,
its shadow crackling restless as though
agitated or startled and trying to run away.

A loving father stands over his daughter.
His shadow descends on her at play
like a protective veil hiding curls and swirls.

A bird flies between a man and the sun,
its shadow shudders, circles around again
as though it's a spy plane not a hawk.

The moon squeezes between sun and earth
shadows made of disks and living crescents,
white-hot-sun waits like a crowbar to retina pry.

I stand in an August heat-basted midday glare,
my hand held high, casting a shadow over my eyes.
Shadow has told my head to grab the day.

Previews of Coming Attractions

My next poem is going to go pyrotechnic,
combustible like solstice boats Susan and I
build yearly with jellied alcohol, 4th of July
sparklers, and pop bottle rockets. Little notes mark
"Bad things of the year" to be purified by pagan fire.
Race between my peeking eyes and fire's flames.

My next poem is going to have big "mood hats"
so you can understand by sight why a wife with GI
helmet tells you by sight she is getting ready for expected abuse,
beanie hatted son—hunkering down Spanish American history.
Hat outfitted with spinners and twirlers—ready for either
Barnum & Bailey carnival or an epoch breakthrough in fly-fishing.

My next poem will be x-rated, banner phrases provocatively
flying—"Love the twisted as much as the bloody mess of it,"
"Pull me hard and get me straight," "Twist it a little, but not so
much it will fall out," "If I had a set of balls like that, I'd join the
circus." Set your imagination panting, let your pulse rate climb,
only to discover I'm writing about Prego spaghetti and meatballs.

My next poem is going to lick and seal labels laced with
Viagra so tongues go rigid and poke out of mouths like lollipops,
Valium to chill out lick by lick so after the third lick the letter
holder thinks seriously about getting inside—posting themselves.
Thorazine on the label—Sylvia Plath take your head out of the
oven, extinguish the match and turn off the gas. Go electric!

A final poem will include a confidentiality agreement template
with "I agree" provision so you sign it first, then read. Intellectual
property protected because I'm going to tell you a terrible secret.

About the Author

Terry Brix, a green chemical engineer who lives in Blue River, Oregon, divides his time between two careers: writing poetry, novels, and memoir, and developing green sustainable projects with countries such as Norway, Finland, Iceland, South Africa, United States and Canada. Brix's poetry walks hand-in-hand with science, technology and his international interests and passions. Inspired by his travels to Norway where he was astounded by Oslo's Vigeland Sculpture Park, he created *Chiseled from the Heart,* a poetry collection celebrating the genius of Gustav Vigeland, which was published in 2000 by Vigeland Museum.

His poetry has appeared in, among others, *Dos Passos Review, Concho River Review, The Evansville Review, Fireweed, Curbside Review, Rattlesnake Review, The Antioch Review* and *North American Review.*

Fighting Exile, started in 2012 during a month-long fellowship residency at Playa, reflects on the diverse feelings surrounding his exile from his beloved Montana where he was born and raised. He is currently working on new poetry collections, juxtaposing international topics and themes with his western poetic focus on Montana, Oregon and the Pacific Northwest.

www.terrybrix.com